Hidden Around Imagination. What you see is what you color

HAI™

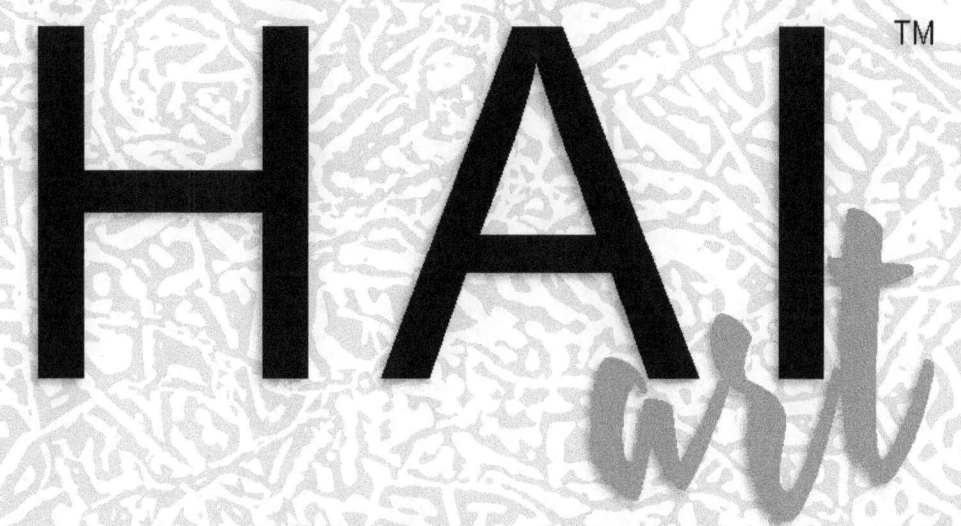

Created by J.K. Shin

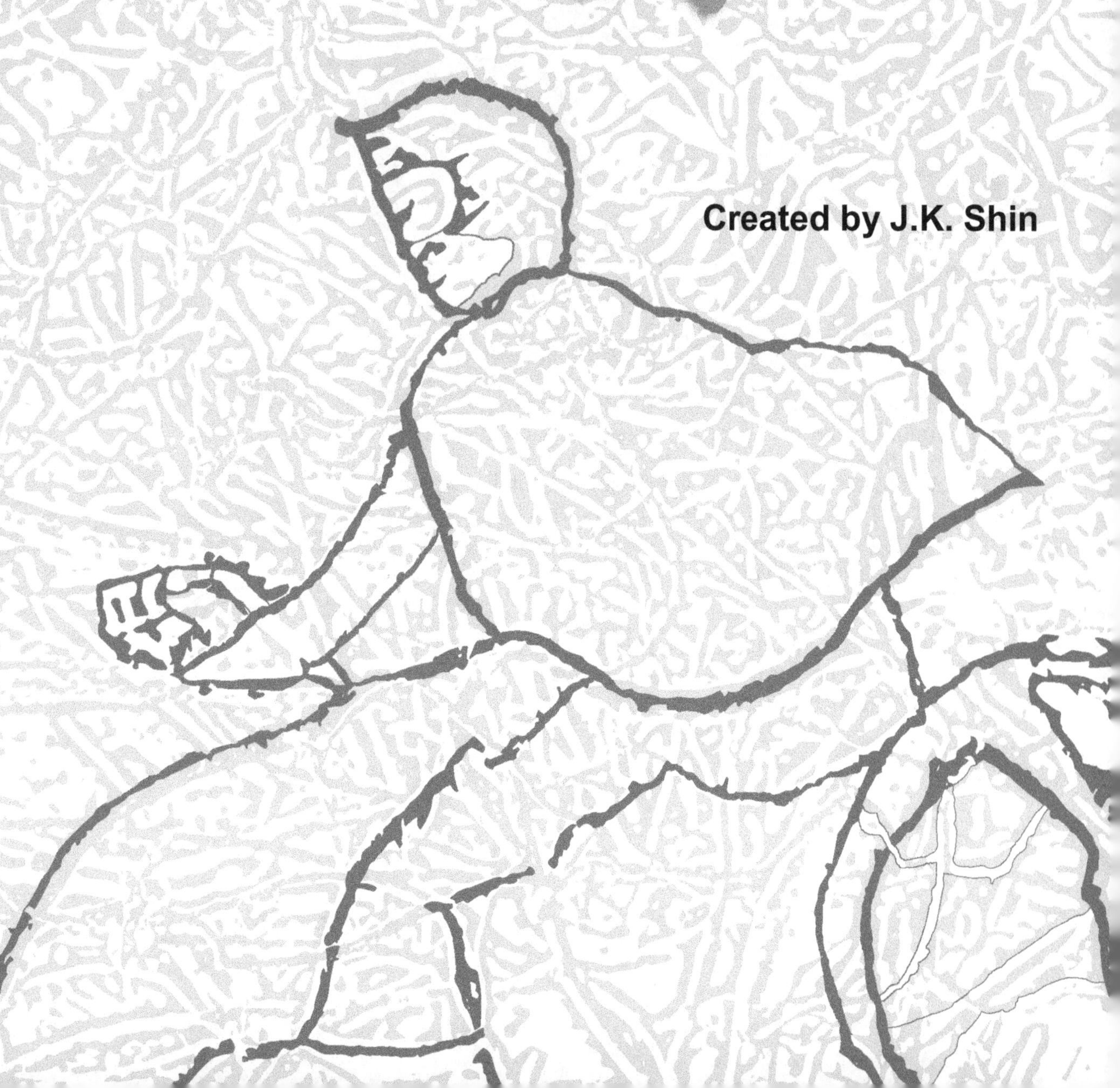

HAIart

Copyright © 2019 by J.K. Shin

ISBN 978-1-5136-5372-3

For information about custom editions, special sales, and premium and corporate purchases, please contact haiart.co@gmail.com.

www.HAIart.co

CREATE YOUR OWN

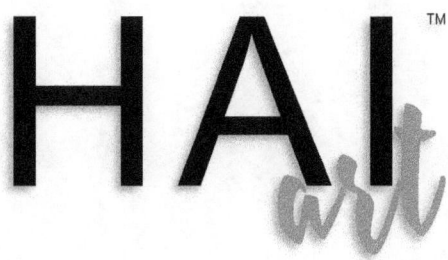

"Hidden Around Imagination" or HAIart leverages abstract designs and fractals to let your creativity run wild. Unlike traditional coloring books where you fill in pre-determined drawings, HAIart is open-ended where fractals inspired by nature lets you decipher and illustrate your perceptions, like looking at mysterious ink blot or abstract cloud shapes.

STEP 1: Use the fractals in this book to open up your imagination.

STEP 2: There is no "right" way to see images on the fractals. Turn the paper sideways or upside down for more inspiration and relax your eyes to see the bigger picture.

STEP 3: Take a pen or pencil and draw in the outline of what you see. The possibilities are endless.

STEP 4: Color in your vision with colored pencils, crayons, markers, or your favorite coloring medium.

STEP 5: Take a picture of your final image and share it on social media with #HAIartlife and explore other creations.

STEP 6: Follow @haiartlife on Instagram, Twitter, and Facebook. and sign up for new fractals on haiart.co.

STEP 7: HAIart is also great for cultivating children's creativity.

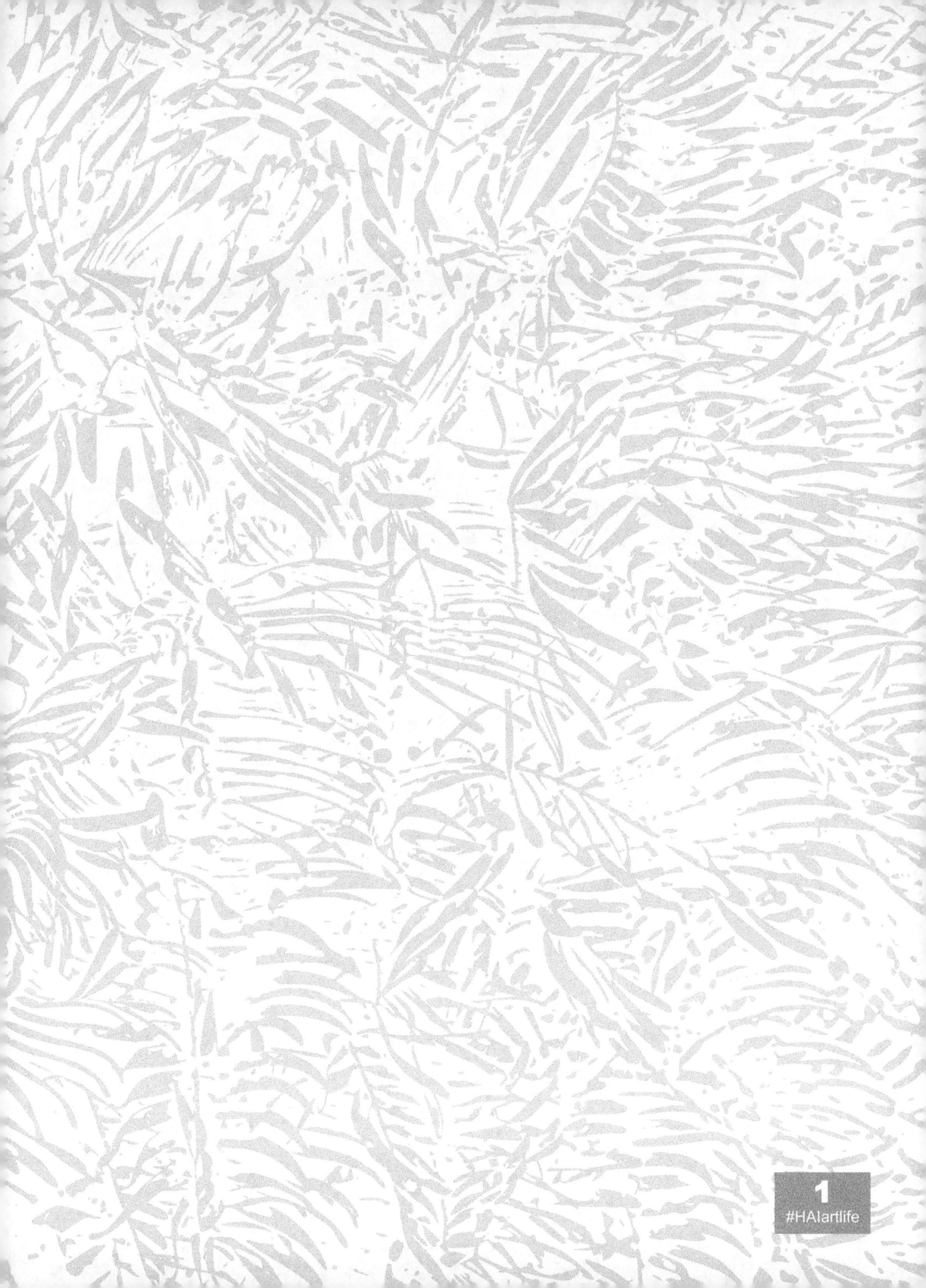

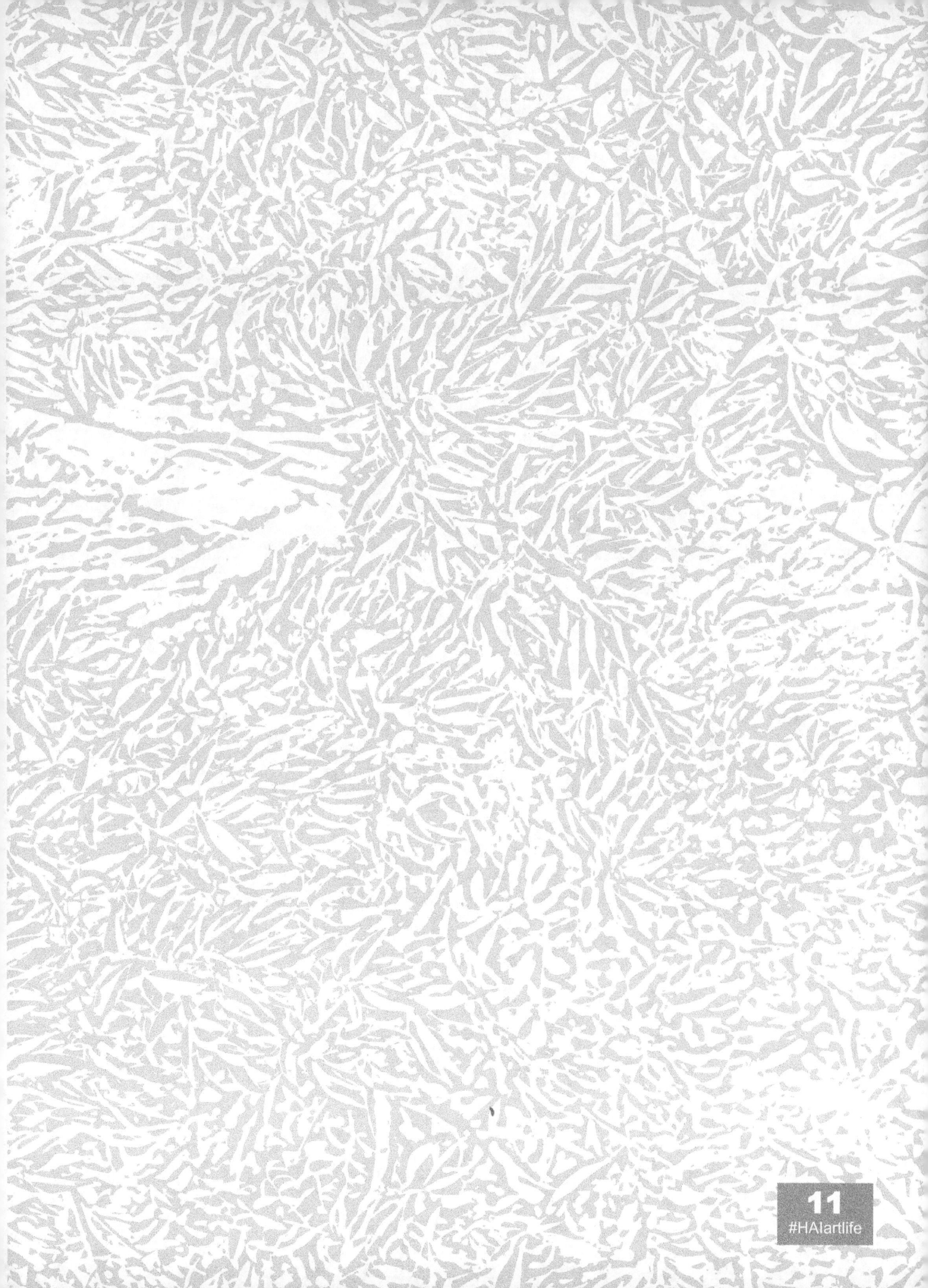

11
#HAIartlife

13
#HAIartlife

17
#HAIartlife

www.ingramcontent.com/pod-product-compliance
Lightning Source LLC
Chambersburg PA
CBHW080618180526
45168CB00007B/2968

* 9 7 8 1 5 1 3 6 5 3 7 2 3 *